GERARD YAO

UNDERSTANDING MONEY

The Ultimate Guide on Money Making Methods,
Learn Different Ways and Effective Strategies
of Making Money Anywhere

Descrierea CIP a Bibliotecii Naționale a României
GERARD YAO
UNDERSTANDING MONEY. The Ultimate Guide on Money Making Methods, Learn Different Ways and Effective Strategies of Making Money Anywhere / Gerard Yao – Bucharest: Editura My Ebook, 2021
    ISBN

GERARD YAO

UNDERSTANDING MONEY
The Ultimate Guide on Money Making Methods,
Learn Different Ways and Effective Strategies
of Making Money Anywhere

My Ebook Publishing House
Bucharest, 2021

TABLE OF CONTENT

Introductory 7

Chapter 1: Options To Make Money Online 9

Chapter 2: Top Ways To Make Money Online 12

Chapter 3: Does Money Make Money? 16

Chapter 4: Easy Ways To Make Money 21

Chapter 5: Essential Tips To Make Money At Home 24

Chapter 6: Ways for a Kid to Make Money 27

Chapter 7: Will I make money online? 32

INTRODUCTORY

Can you believe I spent close to 1 year searching for work at home ideas and opportunities to make money from?

There are tons of information being presented to you through all sorted of money making programs.

I have joined many programs and purchased many e-books about money making online. After spending up to $5000 I feel like I am just spinning the wheels and still getting nowhere.

I can't tell you how many mindless hours I've spent sitting in front of my computer trying to make money online and still get nowhere. Sounds familiar? I bet it does.

I don't know about you, but I've spent a lot of money in the past. The one thing you should know is that making money on the Internet will only be limited by one thing – your time.

Recently, I was introduced by my mentor about a book called "Multiple streams of Income" by bestselling author,

Robert Allen. In the book talked about the necessity for people to create multiple streams of income.

So, when I read through the PlugInProfit make money online program website. I was extremely exciting to know about this program that's helping people like YOU and me to make money online by joining different programs with your own website. At last, I can concentrate to promote only ONE website with multiple streams of income.

I don't want you to make the same mistake I did because as an online marketer, we need to concentrate on ONE marketing website rather than promoting different affiliate programs each time.

A lot of my time is taking up. You can avoid many costly pitfalls and dramatically accelerate your path to profits online.

Then What Should the Internet Marketer Do?

The Key is to stay focused.

Success can be yours as long as you have the patience and persistence to ACT on the steps outlined for you. Remember, in this internet business, it is not a race. It is a journey.

Chapter 1

Options To Make Money Online

With technology so advanced and everything available with the click of your mouse, you can even make money online from your home, with little or no investment and with a basic working knowledge of the computer.

Stock market online

For those who are interested in keeping abreast of stocks and shares, this awareness could be utilized to make money online. Stocks and shares are escalating or deteriorating in prices on an almost daily basis, and is you keep up with the stock market news, you will have an idea of how things will be in the near future.

Buying and selling according to the rise and fall in the prices could make you wealthy in a short while. Even payment for the shares that you have bought could be done online and you could transfer money to or from you bank for such payments. With this business acumen of stocks and shares you can make money online and that too a sizable amount.

There is a lot of information on the news channels and on the internet about the stock rates and all you have to do is to follow the trends of the stock market and do your buying and selling accordingly. If you want to make money online, stocks and shares is the most exciting way to do it.

Conduct online classes and make money online

Adult education is a very active part of the teaching line now. Many people have had to give up their education midway and would love to continue where they left off, but find it difficult because of time constraints. They now hold jobs, have families to support and maintain their homes. For such persons it would be a major boon if they could continue their education online.

On the other side of the coin is the teaching online which would help them. If you are interested in the teaching line and if you have the necessary qualifications, you could help these persons by teaching them online. There are many educational institutes online that cater to online students. As a teacher you could register with them and conduct your classes online and make money online.

Here again, the student and the teacher can be at different ends of the globe and communicate on the net. If you want to have flexible work timings you could be a teacher online, classes will be conducted via the internet and both the student and the teacher benefit from this. The student gains knowledge and the teacher get job satisfaction and also could make money online.

Set examination papers online for various institutes

An offshoot of the teaching line is setting examination question papers for universities and other institutes. Many institutes hire persons to write these question papers for them and pay them accordingly; this is one more way of make money online. There will be deadlines to maintain and dates to stick to, but the work is conducted online and you can make money online.

Like in teaching, the person who is setting the paper and institute asking for it can be in two completely different parts of the world. They come together for this purpose via the internet and payment and other issues are all handled online.

Chapter 2

Top Ways To Make Money Online

Why would anyone want to make money online? Well, firstly you can work from anywhere in the world that you can get an internet connection.

Secondly, you can create an incredible income even if you only have a few hours a day. So, if you want freedom, flexibility and want to make money, read on…

So, how do you actually make money online?

Here are some of the most popular and proven ways to make money online, in no particular order:

1. Make money on eBay
2. Make money with blogs
3. Make money with Online Surveys
4. Affiliate Marketing
5. Google AdWords

6. Google AdSense
7. Your own website

Some of these methods require some internet knowledge, while some are suitable for a total beginner. Some will produce an immediate income while others may take months or more.

For instance, blogs and surveys are ideal for the beginner, and surveys can produce immediate income. A blog is like an online journal. Surveys simply require you to share your opinion.

Your own web-site on the other hand requires some expertise and will usually produce income in the longer-term. However, once your site does start making money for you, it's like having your own money-printing machine!

Google AdSense is where you enable adverts to show on your blog or website, and you get paid every time someone clicks on the ads. So, if your blog or website become popular, and you are getting thousands of visitors a week or a day, you can make a great income doing pretty much nothing! (You did the work previously setting up the blog or site and now you can reap the rewards).

Google AdWords is where you pay for your own advert that will appear down the right side of the page when people do a google search. For instance, let's say you are selling health products and need more customers. If you have your own website, however simple, you can create an advert that will appear on Google's search results when someone does a search for health products.

You pay every time someone clicks on your advert. Let's say Google charge you 20 cents a click, and for every 30 people that click you get a sale of, say, $40. As long as you are in profit with the results, it can be well worth doing. However, I strongly recommend that you follow the experts with this method, else you could waste a lot of money.

Affiliate marketing can work well with AdWords. This is where you send buyers to other people's websites and get generous commission on any sales made. The sales are tracked by way of a coded link. You don't need to buy stock or send items to customers, the website owner does all that. This can be a superb way to make money once you understand it.

Selling on eBay is another way to make money online quickly. You don't need to sell stuff from your loft, you can sell whatever you are most interested in – so, if you love sport, why not look into selling sports-related items. If you make jewelry, sell that. If you love dogs, sell dog-related items. Again, there are tricks of the trade that will make the difference between eBay success and failure.

There are e-books available which show you how to create your own web- site and you can also get free websites when you buy information packages on the web (for examples of this visit the recommended businesses via the link below). I make money in all these areas because I think it's a great idea to have more than one income stream. After all, why limit yourself?

My best advice is to do what I did and copy those who are already making money online as I demonstrate in the e-book. Why? Well, you can avoid wasting lots of time and money this way. I spent 18 months trying to figure out the best ways to make money online and the result is, many methods can work but not always as fast as you may wish. So, you can get started with the methods that make immediate cash and then progress into other methods if you want to earn more.

Some people make six figures A MONTH online, while others just want a few hundred a week. That's the great thing about making money online, you can build up to whatever income you want, and let's face it, there aren't many jobs that offer you that!

Chapter 3

Does Money Make Money?

If you write articles for your website, try not to include the affiliate links in the body of your articles: it will give the impression that you have a vested interest in recommending them.

You want your visitors to trust your advice, so don't turn your article into an excuse to promote products and make a commission.

Christian home-based business called Disciple's Cross. With Disciple's Cross, you make beautiful crosses and send these crosses back to the company.

The company will pay you for the crosses it accepts. It has been a lot of fun to participate in this business opportunity and wonderful ministry.

Instead of buying links, get one-way links from blog search engines and directories, as well as getting your RSS feed content displayed at other sites.

Does Money Make Money?

If it is your goal to accumulate wealth, believing the fallacy that money makes money, will hinder your progress to no end. This belief stifles many to a life of failure, and misery.

The goal setting theory of motivation means that you need to be positive - and realistic - to be able to reach your goal, especially if that goal is to make money.

How many times do we hear that "money makes money." Money can make money just as easily as Ferrari can win the Grand Prix without Schumaker in the driver's seat.

"Ferrari is the Grand Prix world champion." Do we say that? "Microsoft invented Windows." Do we say that? Or do we say, "Schumaker is the world champion." And "Gates invented Windows."? Of course, we give credit to the person, or people. And that's because that is the reality.

Money is an innate, lifeless thing. To illustrate...

Let's say we want to make our money grow, then we place a $100 note in a tin and bury it, and a year later we return and dig it up. How much money will there be? Only our $100 note we placed in the tin. There is no way, on God's green earth that there can be one cent more than the original $100.

Before spending a lot of time and money marketing an affiliate program, always check it out first. There are a number of ways to do this.

If you want to have more money and free time, you must work for it consistently and persistently with

I kept reading over and over again to get your own domain name and create your own web site. Then incorporate all your affiliate links into your new web site. Create a theme and join affiliate programs related to that theme. But I knew nothing about creating a web site. And what the heck is HTML?

The right opportunity until you reach success. Winner will never quit until they are successful.

People make money! And people lose money!

Certainly, money can earn interest, but the person (or rather the person's intelligence) is required to invest the money to earn that interest. In this regard, a person can make a bad investment, and not earn as much interest, or can lose money.

On the other side of the coin (no pun intended), a person can indulge in a business venture, and this way make money. Or lose it!

Whichever route is taken, it is the intelligence of the PERSON that either makes money, or makes more money. This is the way it has always worked, and always will.

Even in the event where someone has a big windfall, like winning the lottery, this money can be squandered, or made to multiply. Whichever it is, it is up to the person, to either invest wisely, or to spend endlessly. The history books are full of tales where enormous fortunes were won, and then lost.

Therefore, if it is your goal to make money, don't fall into the trap of believing that "money makes money"; it is a lifeless object, that cannot possible multiply without the intelligence of a human being. Rather...

Make it your goal to...

... learn about money, and how to invest and use it to multiply.

I do not remember how I got started but after a while I started searching for money earning opportunities on the net. I would sit and search for long hours every day. I would search till my eyes get sore. I was wasting my time but I did not know. Every day I would search and click new sites. Making money ideas by Victoria, Duvet Dollars. See my Duvet Dollars review here!

With Google AdWords advertising program, you can make your ad show-up when somebody types in these terms... and you don't even need your own product. There are thousands of retailers that offer you up to 70% commission for every product you sell.

With so many ways to make money online, what is the best way to work from the comfort of your own home without breaking a sweat?

Chapter 4

Easy Ways To Make Money

There are easy ways to make money in my opinion, but of course this means different things to different people.

For example, do you want easy ways to make money right now, or ways to make the most over time with the least effort? These really are two very different things.

Easy Ways To Make Money Right Now

Go get a job. Or just work more hours at your present job. Starting a business or learning to invest successfully isn't easy. A job is easier. To be able to go to work and get a paycheck every week or two guaranteed - that's easy!

Sell things. An easy way to make money quickly is to sell whatever you don't need. Get rid of the second car, the boat you never use, etc.

Reduce expenses. Stop smoking, and learn how to spend less for all the things you buy. If you can spend $14 less each day on unimportant things, you save over $5,000 per year. That's like making $7,000 more (you have to earn that much to have $5,000 after taxes).

Easy Ways To Make Money - Eventually

The job is easier than a business, but really only in the near-term. If you define easy as "the most money over time for the least effort," you need to invest or start a business, or both. I've got two stories to demonstrate that idea.

I bought my first home in my twenties, and it was just a mobile home on real estate, but I discovered that I could easily rent rooms. I was soon living for free as well as banking some of the money.

This wasn't a "get rich quick" scheme, but I made as much as $7,000 per year extra from my investment. I had to work to pay off the mortgage, but in the end, I was working much less than my friends were.

My second story has to do with this internet business. I spend a lot of time writing these articles now, and distributing them. People read them, click through to my web sites from the link at the bottom, and maybe buy a product that I get a commission on, or I get paid for the advertising clicks. Really, it is pretty easy now, but that's not how it started.

I worked full time from the start. Six months into it, I was making a net profit of about $2 per day. It was a bit discouraging. I had a lot to learn. Fortunately, I learned my lessons, and as it turns out, I was making something closer to $30 per hour for my time.

I just wouldn't be paid for the first year. Now the business pumps out the money I made from those earlier efforts, and keeps doing so even when I am on vacation.

That's the way it is with money. If you want more money than a job will provide, you have to invest or start a business. That may mean you work for a dollar per hour to start, so that you can easily collect $100 per hour, years down the road. If that sounds too discouraging, then maybe there are no easy ways to make money.

Chapter 5

Essential Tips To Make Money At Home

Great ideas that will help you start to make money at home without any hassles. Get all the inside scoop on money making opportunities!

Being a stay at home can be tough. Not only do you have to spend most of your time indoors but also have to give up on the prospect of a career. Well, if you wish to enjoy the best of both worlds, you can do so now by learning how to make money at home.

Franchising

If you love to promote products and services and have a knack of selling, then this job is for you. You can easily avail a variety of franchising work opportunities at your disposal. The way it works is that the franchisor or company will provide you access to all the training, support and information needed to market their products and services. Then you the franchisee needs to sell these products.

The reason why franchising is great to make money at home is because of the tremendous flexibility it provides. You not only get to choose the timings of your job but also the amount of work you wish to take on at a stretch. Not just that, with franchising you can make money at home without having to search for suppliers or advertising material to market the business.

Everything is provided to you as part of the package. Thus, franchising essentially provides you the same feeling of having your own business – without the added hassles. Through franchising you can easily make money at home in a fast and effective manner.

Aerobics or fitness instructor

If you are a fitness freak and love to stay in shape, then you can easily make money at home by becoming a fitness instructor! Yes, you just need to advertise your services in any of the classifieds. Or if you happen to have your own website, it's even better! You can advertise and publicize your services online. As you gain more popularity you will find more and more people thronging to your classes. What's more later on you could even release videos of workouts or fitness ideas etc. – thereby doubling your chances at income. In today's age where everyone is health conscious being a fitness instructor is probably one of the most sought-after jobs around.

You can also make money at home very quickly.

Hair stylist

If you love fashion and all things that go with it, then being a hair stylist can be a rewarding profession. Not only do you get to experiment with latest styles and fashion trends, you can easily make money at home in substantial amounts. You could start your own hair salon at home and advertise your services online on your website.

Provide innovative tips on having great looking hair etc. which can help establish you as an authority on the subject. This way you'll find more people flocking to your salon and you will get to make money at home easily and effectively.

If you want to learn more, do not hesitate to visit the link attached. You will definitely be satisfied with what you can get from there.

Chapter 6

Ways for a Kid to Make Money

One of the ways for a kid to make money. Can a kid make money by writing essays?

Yes! After 2 years perhaps more than many adults are earning.

Teen Handicaps

- No experience of life
- No money
- Need time for homework, sport and friends.

Teen Advantages

- It's not true that you've no experience. You've a lot of school experience.
- You have a lot more energy to bring to the task than many adults have.

- You can get help. Your English teacher will be delighted to help you with writing essays.
- Parents can pay for ways for a kid to make money. Get their promise to get you started if you get top marks for ten essays. You'll soon write top essays with my free report.
- Time for 2 essays/week.

No Salesmanship

Your ways for a kid to make money must not need salesmanship. As a salesperson you wouldn't be looking for ideas - you'd already be making money.

You really can do it

How do I know? A teenage girl is making money with this idea just writing essays about her holidays. You don't need to know anything about making a web site. The package that Nori uses does all the technical stuff for you. So, there's no excuse... you concentrate on ways for a kid to make money with essays.

Tier 1 of ways for a kid to make money

1. Find a demand. Choose a subject that interests you with lots of popular keywords (search terms).

2. Check Overture for top bids on the most popular keywords. Best if there are lots of keywords with bids over $5.

3. Search Google. If there are 30 million sites competing for a keyword you aren't quite ready to compete.

4. There is a better search tool that does steps 1 and 3 for you but it's not free.

5. The package that Nori uses, has a search engine built in.

Just one word of warning. If you're using Overture keyword tools and suddenly get a message saying that you're over using it - you've lost the use of a tool. Other keyword tools keep changing their IP number so Overture doesn't recognize them on their next visit.

There isn't room here to cover all the ways that I use to discover what people want to read about.

In all ways for a kid to make money the important idea is... avoid selling. You need to sell if there is no interest. If people are interested they'll swarm around you.

You want people who are interested and have money

That's why you check on the top bids. Forget a subject with 5 cent bids. Don't stop until you find a good subject. An unpopular subject will lose you money.

Ways for a kid to make money?

You are ready when…

- Hordes visit your site.
- You've written about 30 popular web pages.

Submit your site to Google AdSense. Once they accept you they'll give you a code to put on your web pages.

Each time someone clicks on an AdSense advert on your page with a $5 bid, Google gets a share and you get a share. Do you see why I don't suggest bothering with 5cent bids? You're getting money without selling anything at all.

Tier 2 of Ways for a Kid to Make Money

Now continue writing more web pages, but also write free articles like this one.

Why...? What's the point...?

- See the links at the foot of this article for free goodies? When your article excites anybody, they visit your website. Thousands of visitors mean thousands of people seeing your AdSense ads, which means...more money.

- You will build your reputation. Reputation is valuable for your future.
- Archive your articles on cheap website offering a sub-domain
- Modify and reuse on your web pages.

Employment

One day you may want a job if you haven't chosen a subject that thrills visitors.

Reputation: your potential employer may have read some of your articles. Otherwise suggest a Google search on a unique phrase in one of your articles. If she sees that 1256 websites have copied your article will she be impressed?

Money: you can afford to wait for a better job if you're getting money from your website.

Experience: how many of your rivals have experience handling money, keeping accounts, filling in tax forms, making a website? Very few I think!

Chapter 7

Will I make money online?

This is the number one question people ask when they are looking for profits on the internet. Will I make money online?

95% of the people who start to look for ways to make money online fail eventually. The classic story is - start looking for information then a flood of misleading information hits you and you drown.

You will try this then try that but fail at all of them and soon you will quit. Just to find yourself in that old crampy day job you wanted to run away from to begin with. Today I will try to stop this and do a little mind arranging and show you one door to success.

I am not intending to prattle here and waste your time, let's get directly to the point. Making money online is actually based on one simple very basic formula:

Find a hungry crowd-> Find what they want -> Give it to them

That's it there you have it, in a nut shell the whole internet marketing big philosophy purified in one short sentence.

OK, you think to yourself this is real nice but how do I manage all this? I will give you one way, among endless ways, to your success today.

But before that you must remember the most important thing in internet marketing:

Whatever it is you choose to do, keep doing it and doing it and doing it. Do not jump from one program to another program, failing them all. Choose one path and keep moving forward, for this is the only way you will ever, manage to make money online.

Now let's break the formula into few basic steps you can start performing today.

Find a hungry crowed

You must find what people are searching for to be able to supply it. This is the "What should I sell online?" question everyone asks. Technically you can use search engines and find popular search terms – but remember to look for something people want but not too popular. Another way is using any free keyword suggestion tool, simply look for these exact words, to find what people are looking for online.

Find what they want

Now you know what people are looking for but what will you give them? Let's say that you have found that people are looking for solution to some medical problem, you can give them information on how to solve their problem or products: pills, instruments, etc.

One more sample: if they are looking for ways to keep their dog from barking, give them a book which tells them exactly how they should train their dog. Finding what they want is all about finding specific solution to a certain problem.

Give it to them

Now you think: I have to look for what people need, find out what can solve their problem and then give it to them. But how will I find it? I don't have it at home, or at my car. Should I start create solutions? Writing a book? Build a real sophisticated machine? No, you don't!!! This part is actually taken care for you, along with the entire customer handling.

The answer is Affiliates programs. They are free to join. And you will find almost anything you can think of. They take care of creating, shipping, and customer support for you. All you need is to bring home the hungry crowd in because dinner is already served!

www.ingramcontent.com/pod-product-compliance
Ingram Content Group UK Ltd.
Pitfield, Milton Keynes, MK11 3LW, UK
UKHW022213230426
12048UKWH00016BA/827